THE GREAT WALL

GU BEIKOU - JIN SHANLING - SI MATAI
PHOTO BY ZHOU WANPING

我 的 家 乡

古北口 —— 金山岭 —— 司马台

Zhou wan ping

周万萍摄影

2011.04.17.

中国摄影出版社

图书在版编目(CIP)数据

我的家乡 / 周万萍摄影

—北京:中国摄影出版社,1999.12

ISBN 7-80007-333-5

Ⅰ.我… Ⅱ.周… Ⅲ.摄影集-中国-现代 Ⅳ.J421

中国版本图书馆CIP数据核字(1999)第72779号

责任编辑:陈瑾

翻译:郭晓光(英文)陈诤(日文)王琼(法文)

美术设计:陈鹏

我的家乡

周万萍摄影

出版:中国摄影出版社(东单红星胡同61号)

制版印刷:北京雅昌彩色印刷有限公司

发行:新华书店北京发行所

开本:787×1092 1/12

印张:7

版次:2000年1月第一版 2000年1月第一次印刷

2005年3月第二版 2005年3月第二次印刷

印数:5000-15000册

ISBN 7-80007-333-5/J.333

定价:118元

序 *PREFACE*

每个人都有出生地,并且都有自己的童年和成长史,这本精美的摄影画册不仅描述了金山岭、司马台、古北口长城的宏伟与壮丽,同时也折射着一个青年农民转变为职业摄影师的故事。

可以说,二十年前周万萍还是一个不太懂事的孩子,外面的世界是个什么样子,他几乎是一无所知,只是后来金山岭长城的开放,亲眼看到许多外来的摄影师在金山岭所拍得的作品,使他从另一个角度认识了这里的长城,并重新认识了自我。所以,甚至可以说"一不小心"就拿起照相机,把祖祖辈辈对这里的一切情感集中在照相机的镜头上,对准这里长城上的一砖一瓦,一草一木……。如今,他多次站在领奖台上,感受国内、国际送给他的各种殊荣,而每幅获奖作品拍摄的却都是他家乡的万里长城。就此,一个"家乡的父老乡亲,祖国的山山水水,世界的文化遗产",永远铭刻在他的心里。

周万萍的文化程度并不高,身体还有些残疾,是勤奋给他创造了更多的机遇,是艰辛给他带来了更深沉的思考,然而又是大家的鼓励给他增添了更大的力量。我以为在众多喜欢拍摄长城的摄影家中,周万萍所拍摄的日出、日落最多,拍摄的彩虹最多,当然,似乎也可以断言,他失败的次数同样也最多,但他从不气馁,总是朝着更新更高的目标迈去。周万萍没有上过专门的摄影学校,更没有大学文凭,他只是把许许多多来这里拿照相机的游客和摄影师统统视为自己的老师。日复一日,年复一年,万里长城成为周万萍了解世界和领悟人生的大课堂。

周万萍作为摄影人第一个在金山岭的小金山上手持海鸥相机拍下了成名之作《云雾锁长城》,然后,他又毫无保留地把这个拍摄角度告诉了许多摄影者。如今只要是有云雾的清晨,那个只有十几平米的山头上摆放的全是三角架,包括我在内,也曾在这里等候着云雾出现的奇观。

啊!这就是周万萍家乡的金山岭!

这就是中国的万里长城!

Everyone has his birthplace, childhood as well as his own story of success. In this exquisite photo album, pictures about different parts of the Great Wall at the Jin Shan Mount, Si Ma Tai and Gu Bei Kou sites show how a young farmer became a professional photographer.

20 years ago, Mr. Zhou Wanping, then a little boy had almost no knowledge at all about the rest of the world outside the mountains.After the Great Wall at the Jin Shan Mount became a scenic site, Mr. Zhou Wanping began to look at the Great Wall as well as himself from a different angle. He met foreign phtographers and saw their pictrues of the Great Wall . Later, he"picked up"the art of photography. He took pictures of ancient bricks and broken tiles, a reflection of his love for his hometown. Today, standing on the platform to receive prizes in photography contests, he knows that all his affection will never change for his hometown at the Great Wall, his fellow villagers and his beloved motherland.

Mr. Zhou Wanping, slightly handy-capped,didn't receive any college education. Rather than that, he was self-made through hard working.Encouragement from friends has helped him for further achievement. Compared to other photographers, who love to picture the Great Wall, Zhou's camera focuses more on the sun rising ,sun setting and the rainbows on the Great Wall,

Of course, that means more failures than others,though that never stop him.Instead,he works harder for the better. Zhou never has the chance to study in any institutions of photograhpy, not mention any diplomas from college. Tourists with cameras and the professional photographers coming to the Great Wall have become his handy teachers. Day in day out,the Great Wall is the best classroom for Zhou to learn about the world and about the life.

Zhou first came to fame for his photo entitled"Clouds over the Great Wall", taken with a Sea Gull camera on the Jin Shan Mount. Later, he told many photographers the location. Now,the location is crowed with tripods on misty mornings.I myself once went there,waiting for a foggy view of the Great Wall.

This is the Jin Shan Mount,hometown of Mr.Zhou Wanping. This is the Great Wall that extends ten thousands li.

国の山と川のすべて、世界の文化遺産」は永遠は心の中に深く銘記している。

　周万萍さんの文化水準はそんなに高くない、且つ身体障害でもある。しかし、勤勉は彼により多くのチャンスを与え、苦難は彼により多くの思考をもたらし、特に囲りの励ましはより大きな支えを添えた。長城を撮影した多くの写真家に、周万萍さんは日の出、日没と虹を最も多くとった。当然失敗の回数も最も多いと断言できる。でも彼はすこしも諦めず、ずっとより新しい、より高い目標を目差して努力している。周万萍さんは専門の撮影学校に入ったこともないし、大学卒業証明までもない。彼は長城にくるカメラを持っ観光客と写真家がすべて自分の先生だと見なしている。一日にまた一日、一年また一年にして、万里の長城は周万萍さんの世界を理解し、人生を会得する大きな教室となった。

　周万萍さんは写真家として、初めて金山嶺の小さい山の上で、カモメ印のカメラで名をなす作品《長城、雲、霧》をとった。その後、彼は少しも残ずに、この写真をとるアングルなどを多くの写真家に披露した。今になると、雲と霧の朝に、この十数平方メートルの山の上に、三脚はいっぱい置いてある。私までもここで雲と霧の中の奇麗な眺めを待っていた。

　ああ、ここは周万萍さんの故里である金山嶺。ここは中国の万里の長城。

人には出生地があり、且つ自分の幼年と成長史がある。この精緻で美しい写真集は金山嶺、司馬台、古北口長城の雄大と壮麗を述べただけでなく、一人の青年農民からプロの写真家に脱皮する物語を屈折している。

　20年前、周万萍さんはまだ物知らぬ子供だった。外の世界がどういうものか、彼には全然分からなかった。後の金山嶺長城の開放によって、この目で見た外来の写真家たちの金山嶺で撮った作品は彼をもう一つの角度からこの長城を認識させ、自分を新たに認識するようになった。だから「うっかりして」カメラをとって、先祖代々の長城への愛情をレンズに収め、焦点を長城のレンガ、瓦、草、木……にあてたとひいて言えるだろう。今になって、彼は何度も受賞の台に立って、国内、海外からいろんな特別な栄誉を感じとるが、毎回の受賞作品は必ず故郷の長城である。これで、「故里の年輩同郷、祖

Chacun a son lieu de naissance, son enfance et son histoire de réussite. Ce bel album raconte la magnificence de la Grande Muraille Jinshanling, Simatai et Gubeikou, lieu de naissance d' un jeune paysan, Monsieur Zhou Wanping et trace son parcours d' un homme des champs à un photographe professionnel.

Il y a vingt ans, le petit Zhou Wanping ne connaissait presque rien sur le monde extérieur en dehors des montagnes où il vivait. C' était avec l' ouverture au grand public de la Grande Muraille Jinshanling et la rencontre avec des photographes et leurs oeuvres qu' il a redécouvert cette Muraille et un autre lui. Il a pris par hasard un appareil-photo et y a mis depuis lors toutes ses passions et amours en visant les briques et les pierres, les herbes et les arbres de la Grande Muraille. Il est déjà maintes fois monté sur les scènes nationales et internationales pour recevoir des prix aux différents concours photographiques. Mais le sujet de ses oeuvres reste toujours le même : la Grande Muraille de son pays natal. Il garde toujours dans son coeur les gens de son village, les montagnes et eaux de sa patrie, et le patrimoine mondial.

Il n' a pas reçu l' éducation supérieure et a même une gêne physique. C' est la diligence qui lui a apporté des opportunités. C' est le travail qui lui a appris à réfléchir. C' est dans les encouragements de ses chers et ses amis qu' il a trouvé la confidence et la force. Parmi autant de photographes qui ont un engoument pour la Grande Muraille, M. Zhou a pris plus de vues du lever et coucher du soleil et d' arc-en-ciel qu' autrui et a sûrement connu plus d' échecs. Mais il n' a jamais renoncé et grimpe toujours vers l' endroit plus haut. Sans diplôme d' éducation supérieure ni expériences dans aucune école photographique, M. Zhou prend tous les touristes avec appareil-photo ou photographes qu'il peut rencontrer pour ses professeurs. Jour après jour, d' année en année, la Grande Muraille devient une grande école pour lui de connaître le monde extérieur et de comprendre la vie.

Il est le premier photographe à prendre la vue de la Muraille sous des nuages à partir de la Colline Petit Jinshan. C' était son premier grand succès pris avec un appareil très rudimentaire de marque Haiou. Et sans la moindre réserve il a présenté à d'

autres photographes cet unqiue angle de vue, un petit terrain précieux d' une dizaine de mètres carrés sur lequel s' entassent maintenant plein de trépieds tous les matins quand il y a du brouillard pour attendre la merveille. J' ai .été là aussi.

C' est la Grande Muraille Jinshanling du pays natal de Zhou Wanping!

C' est la Grande Muraille de la Chine!

2000年1月 北京
Chen Changfen
2000.1. Beijing

united nations educational, scientific and cultural organization
organisation des nations unies pour l'éducation, la science et la culture

7, place de Fontenoy, 75352 Paris 07-SP
1, rue Miollis, 75732 Paris Cedex 15

telephone: + (33.1) 45.68.49.95
fax: + (33.1) 45.68.57.39
e-mail: a.mclurg@unesco.org

ref: upo/d/amcl/98/009

16 January 1998

Dear Ms Zhou Wanping,

Congratulations! I am very happy to be able to inform you that one of your photographs of the Great Wall in China that you submitted to the International World Heritage Photo Competition has been awarded **second** prize by the Jury.

You have won an intercontinental flight for two persons on Lufthansa airlines with accommodation in a Hilton hotel, along with some pocket money to enable you to enjoy your stay wherever you choose to go. On top, you will also receive some Agfa photographic material and processing.

We received over 49,000 photographs from some 91 countries. The first prize went to Spanish photographer Vicente Peiro Asensio for a particularly sensitive shot of Kathmandu Valley in Nepal.

The organizers of the competition - UNESCO, AGFA and LUFTHANSA - wish to take this opportunity, first of all, to congratulate you warmly on your excellent photograph and, secondly, to thank you for participating in this World Heritage photo competition.

To enable me to put you in contact with the people who will give you the necessary information for your travel, etc., I would be grateful if you could confirm your exact address (and telephone or fax number) as soon as possible.

Yours sincerely,

Alastair McLurg
UNESCO Publishing

Ms Zhou Wanping
Luanping County, Hebri
Jingshanling
Great Wall Photography Department
068254 People's Republic of China
作者：周万萍
地址：中国河北省滦平县金山岭长城摄影部
邮编：068254　　电话：0314-8830258

1998年1月在法国巴黎获得联合国举办的"世界文化与自然遗产"摄影比赛二等奖。
January 1998, Paris, France:Second Prize in the"World Culture and Natural Heritage"
1998 年1月に、フランスのパリで国連主催の「世界文化と自然遺産」コンクール二等賞を獲得
1998 janvier : Deuxième prix au Concours photographique international du Patrimoine mondial organisé par l' UNESCO à Paris en France

1992年6月获中、日大自然摄影比赛优秀奖。
June 1992, China：Outstanding Prize in Sino—Japanese Nature Photography Contest
1992 年 6 月　中日大自然写真コンクール優秀賞を獲得
1992 juin : Prix d' Excellence au Concours photographique de Nature sino-japonnais

1997年6月入选新加坡影艺研究会第15届国际艺术摄影展览。
June 1997，Singapore：selected into the 15th International Artistic Photography Exhibition
1997 年 6 月　シンガポール影芸研究会第 15 回国際芸術写真展に入選
1997 juin : Selectionné à 15ème Exposition internationale d' Art photographique organisée par
l' Association d' Art photographique du Singapore

1993年7月获"宝丰杯"全国摄影大赛金牌奖。
July 1993，China ：Gold Prize in the Bao Feng
Cup National Photography Contest
1993 年 7 月 「宝豊杯」全国写真コンクール金メダル
を獲得
1993 juillet : Prix d' Or au Concours national
photographique de Coupe Baofeng

1994年1月获"中国山水风光游"中、日摄影大赛金奖。
January 1994，China：Gold Prize in Sino-
Japanese"China Tour" Photography Contest
1994 年 1 月 「中国山水風光遊」中日写真コンクール
金賞を獲得
1994 janvier : Prix d' Or au Concours sino-japonnais
photographique de Tour de Chine

1994年8月获第17届全国摄影艺术展览金牌奖。
August 1994，China：Gold Prize in 17th National
Photography Contest
1994 年 8 月　第 17 回全国写真芸術展金メダルを獲得
1994 août : Prix d'Or au 17ème Concours et Exposition
d' Art photographique de Chine

1995年4月获"95 适马杯"中国风情全国摄影大奖赛优异奖

April 1995, China：Excellent Prize in"'95 Shi Ma Cup"China Scenery Photography Contest

1995 年 4 月 「95 適馬杯」中国風情全国写真コンクール特別優秀賞を獲得

1995 avril : Prix d' Excellence au Concours photographique du Paysage de Chine de Coupe Shima de 95

1995年6月获"爱克发摄影比赛"优秀奖

June 1995, China：Excellent Prize in Agfa Photograhpy Contest

1995 年 6 月 「愛克発写真コンクール」優秀賞を獲得

1995 juin : Prix d' Excellence au Concours photographique Agfa

1997年12月获97中国旅游年"万事达长城杯"全国摄影大赛特等奖

Dec 1997, Awarded the special prize of the "MAST Card CUP" National Photographic Contest at 97' China Travel Year

1997 年 12 月 97 中国観光年 「マスター杯」全国写真コンクール特別賞を獲得

1997 décembre : Prix spécial au Concours national photographique de Coupe Grande Muraille de MAST de l' Année touristique chinoise de 1997

云飘雾绕
Clouds
雲に漂われ、霧に包まれ
Nuages et fumées

金山岭晨雾
Morning Mist on the Jin Shan Mount
金山嶺の朝霧
Brume matinale sur les Collines Jinshanling

雾弥漫
Mist
霧もうもう
Brouillard

司马台云海
Sea of Clouds over the Si Ma Tai
司馬台の雲海
Mer de nuages sur la Terrasse Simatai

飘缈的雾
Mist
ふんわりとする霧
Brouillard insaisissable

雨后的早晨
Morning after Rain
雨あがりの朝
Matin après la pluie

烟云
Clouds
煙雲
Fumées

黎明
Dawn
夜明け
Aube

翻滚的雾
The Rolling Mist
立ちのぼる霧
Tourbillon de nuages

地势险要
Terrain of Geographic Importance
地勢が険しい
Position stratégique

冬天的曙光
Dawn in Winter
冬の曙
Lueurs de l' aurore en hiver

银装素裹
The Great Wall in Silver
雪の中
La Grande Muraille argentée

初冬
Early Winter
初冬
Début d' hiver

永恒的辉煌
Eternal Glory
永久の輝き
Gloire éternelle

雪后初霁
After Snow
雪あがり
Eclaircie après la neige

岁月
Time
歳月
Temps

随想
Caprice
随想
Caprice

初寒乍暖
Early Winter
初寒ににわかの暖かさ
Premiers jours d' hiver

铜墙铁壁
Fortress
鉄銅の壁
Muraille d' airain

艰巨历程
Hard Times
困難の歩み
Parcours ardu

翻山越岭
Climb over
the Mountains
山を登り峰を越える
Par monts et par vaux

诉说
History
訴え
Raconter

障墙（金山岭）
Fire Wall
障壁（金山嶺）
Mur d' abri

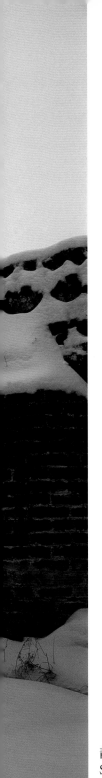

冬日金山岭
Jin Shan Mount in Winter
冬日の金山嶺
Jinshanling en hiver

初雪
First Snow
初雪
Première neige

静静的冬天
Silence in Winter
静かな冬
Hiver figée

单边墙(司马台)
Single Wall
单边壁 (司馬台)
Muraillle unilatérale (Simatai)

长城·朝霞·圆月
The Great Wall, Morning Light and the Moon
長城、朝霞、丸い月
La Grande Muraille, nuages rosés d' aube et la pleine lune

春天的故事
Story of the Spring
春の物語
Histoire du printemps

春之曲
Spring Melody
春の歌
Mélodie du printemps

往事
History
往事
Le passé

杜鹃花盛开的时候
Azalea in Blossom
つつじの咲き乱れる頃
Floraison d' azalées

春意盎然
Spring
春の気配があふれる
Printemps

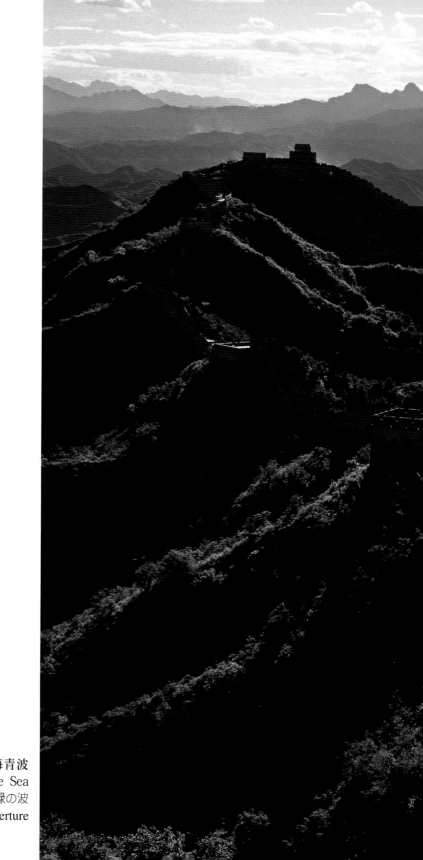

碧海青波
The Sea
青い海緑の波
Mer de verture

太阳雨
Rain
太陽雨
Pluie par soleil

优美的结构
Structure
構造
Structure

彩虹
Rainbow
虹
Arc-en-ciel

小金山楼
（金山岭）
Tower on
the Jin Shan Moun
小金山楼（金山嶺）
Tour de Petit Jinsha
(Jinshanling)

长城进行曲（古北口）
March Melody on the Great Wall
長城進行曲（古北口）
Marche de la Grande Muraille (Gubeikou)

跌宕起伏
Curves
起伏変化に富む
Des hauts et des bas

穿云破雾（库房楼）
Standing in the Clouds
雲を突き抜く霧を破る
Percer les nuages et la brume (Tour d' entrepôt)

金色之晨
Golden Morning
黄金色の朝
Matin doré

宁静的古城
The Quiet Old Town
関所の山はこんなに美しい (古北口)
Ancienne muraille tranquille

关山多娇（古北口）
Mountain View
関所の山はこんなに美しい（古北口）
Montagnes (gubeikou)

古老的长城诉说着无言的历史
History of the Great Wall
古い長城は無言の歴史を語る
Histoire racontée par l' ancienne Muraille

长城·岩石
The Great Wall and
the Rocks
長城、岩石
La Grande Muraille
rochers

晨
Morning
朝
Matin

雨后
After Rain
雨上がり
Après la pluie

古北口
The Great Wall at Gu Bei Kou
古北口
La Grande Muraille Gubeikou

层峦叠嶂
Mountain Ridges
山岳重疊
Superposé

望京楼之夏
Wang Jing Watch Tower in Summer
望京楼の夏
Tour de guet Wangjinglou en été

秋天的诗篇
Poetry in Autumn
秋の歌
Poésie d' automne

金城余辉
Sunset at the Great Wall
夕日の輝き
La Grande Muraille au coucher du soleil

气贯长虹
Significance
意気が虹に届く
Arc-en-ciel sur la Grande Muraille

满城秋色
Autumn
秋は長城に満ちる
Couleurs d' automne

対歌
Aria
語り合う
Aria

高耸入云
Striking into the Sky
雲までそびえる
Elevé au ciel

旭日初升
Sunrise
旭
Lever du soleil

水关（金山岭）
The Great Wall at Shui Guan
水関 (金山嶺)
Passe de l' Eau Shuiguan (Jinshanling)

众志成城
Strong Hold
長々と続く
La volonté de tous

初秋（古北口）
Early Autumn
初秋
Début d' automne

雄风犹存
Magnificence
永遠の威風
Magnificence

天梯（司马台）
The Ladder to the Heaven
天に登る梯子 (司馬台)
Echelle pour le ciel (Simatai)

秋天的呼唤
The Call of the Autumn
秋の呼びかけ
Appel de l' automne

永恒的焦点
Focus on Eternality
恒久の焦点
Foyer pour toujours

往日的回憶
Memory
過ぎし日の追憶
Mémoire

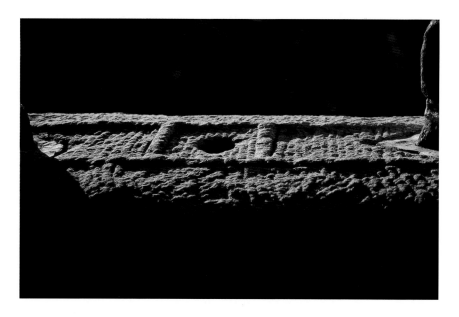

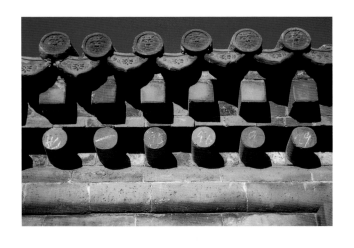

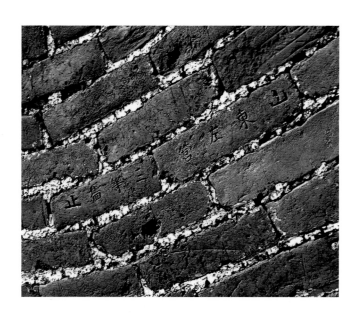

作者像
Portrait of photographer
作者近影

作者全家
The photo of family
私の家族

后记 AFTERWORD

我的家住在金山岭长城脚下二道梁村,坐在家中举头可望见长城的雄姿。在我的童年时代经常听老年人讲起长城的故事。

修建于明代的古北口、金山岭、司马台长城自西向东相连接,全长近30公里,设重要关口12座,峰火台5座,敌楼118座,被誉为长城之最的望京楼海拔986米。这一带长城地势险要,设防严谨,建造艺术精美,宏伟壮观,为古代兵家必争之地。长城以南属北京市密云县,以北为河北省滦平县,我的家在塞外,据村里上了年纪的人讲:我们的村庄历史很久远了,比这里的长城还要早,如今村里居住着30多户人家,大部分都姓周,祖辈靠种田为生。我们家兄弟姐妹6个,我是老二,9岁那年我的左腿严重伤残,1985年我中学毕业回到家,当时,金山岭正在修复之中,我托着病残之躯和民工们一起参加修复长城的劳动。开始懂得了修筑长城工程的浩大与艰难,修长城所用的砖石、石灰、水……,大部分是靠人力背上长城的。有人说:长城是中华民族血汗的结晶。我觉得这是最真实的肺腑之言。

1986年的春天,由于生活所迫,我想到了摄影,花40元钱买了一架旧120海鸥相机,有了它,我欣喜若狂,村里人对我也另眼相看,我就为他们照相,随着长城旅游业的兴起,我就为游客拍照片。

1987年中国的万里长城被列入"世界文化遗产",随即,坐落在我家乡的长城其知名度也越来越高。中、外艺术家纷纷而来创作采风。我结识了摄影界的许多朋友,是他们给了我启发与帮助,我开始试着拍摄长城风光,不久《辽宁青年》杂志封面就发表了我的作品,带着喜悦心情再次登上长城,默想一定要拍摄更多更好的作品,把历史留下的宝贵遗产通过摄影拍摄下来是我的责任,因为我是长城的后代,无论春夏秋冬我始终恪守在长城上,拍摄长城是我一生的夙愿,是长城给了我智慧与力量。我是从一个普通农民的儿子成长为一名职业摄影师的。我在为赞美自己的家乡,弘扬祖国悠久的历史文化努力做着力所能及的事情。为出版这本摄影画册,五年前就有了这个想法,今天终于实现了我的梦想。我认为长城不仅是属于中国的,也是属于世界的。

在本画册出版过程中:承蒙中国摄影家协会领导的关心与帮助;并受到著名摄影家陈长芬先生的厚爱,在编辑过程中陈先生废寝忘食,倾注了大量心血;北京的晶丽达影像图片技术集团;翟东风先生,承德影友衣志坚、李文全先生;承德市教育书店张国先生给予鼎力帮助,长城公司的领导对本画册的出版极为关切;以及在我摄影道路上不断给我注入营养与力量的各界朋友们,在此一并表示衷心的感谢!

I live in a mountain village called Twin Mount Ridges, here one could enjoy the wonderful view of the Great Wall while sitting at home. I have heard so many stories about the Great Wall in my early childhood.

The Great Wall at my hometown was constructed in the Ming Dynasty, running from east to west for over 30 kilometers between Gu Bei Kou and Jin Shan Mount to Si Ma Tai. On this part of the Great Wall, there are 12 key passes, 5 signal smoke towers and 118 combat towers. Among them is the famous Wang Jing Tower, which stands 986 meters above the sea level. The Great Wall here sits on the terrain of geographical importance and was structured for military fortress. The construction looks significant with high level of architectural techniques. All these made it a strategic point in ancient times. Regions south to the Great Wall belong to the Mi Yun County of Beijing, while those north to the Great

Wall are part of the Luan Ping County of He Bei Province. My home village is situated outside the fortress and, according to the older generations, enjoys a history even longer than the Great Wall. Most of the residents in the village share one family name: Zhou and live as farmers for generations. I am the second eldest among the 6 children of my parents. My left leg was severely injured in an accident when I was 9 and I later became crippled. Upon my graduation from middle school in 1985, I returned to the village and participated in the reconstruction of the Great Wall. I witnessed the difficulties during the project in which most of the construction materials were carried onto the wall by manpower. I then understood that wide spread saying here: The Great Wall is constructed with sweat and blood of the Chinese nation. When spring came in 1986, I bought a second-hand SeaGull camera with 40 RMB yuan learn photography to make a living by taking pictures for tourists, I was overjoyed by this change so did the villagers. So I took pictures for them and later in the boom of local tourism for tourists on the Great Wall.

In 1987, the Great Wall included on the list of the World Cultural Heritage. That built up the popularity of the Great Wall and attracted more tourists to my village.

Gradually I made friends with photographers in China and from other countries, They gave me many kind suggestions and inspirations. I started to take pictures of the beautiful views on the Great Wall. Later, my picture became the front cover of a magazine called "Youth in Liao Ning Province" I was so overjoyed that I climbed up the Great Wall and took even more pictures and in different seasons of a year. I consider it my responsibility to preserve the precious heritage by means of photography. This is not only because that I am one of the descendants of the Great Wall, but also that all my power and inspirations come from the Great Wall and made me a professional photographer from a son of an ordinary farmer. I love to walk on top of the Great Wall all year around and take pictures of it for the rest of my life. What I am doing now is what could to praise my hometown and to preserve the historical heritage of my motherland, I had the idea of publishing this photo album 5 years ago and today my dream has become reality. The Great Wall belongs to China and it also belongs to the world.

My heartfelt thanks go to the following for their kind advice and assistance in preparing this photo album; Officials from China Photographers Association; Mr. Chen Changfen, the famous photographer; Mr. Zhai Dongfen, my teacher who introduced me to the art of phototgraphy; Mr. Yi Zhijian and Mr. Li Wenquan from Cheng De City and; management from the Great Wall Corporation.

私は金山嶺長城ふもとの二道梁村に住んでいる。家に座って頭をあげたら、長城雄大の姿が目に入る。幼年時代に年輩者からよく長城の話を聞いた。

明の時代に建築された古北口、金山嶺、司馬台長城は西から東へつないで、長さが30キロに近い。重要な関所12ヵ所、のろし台5ヵ所、見張る望楼118ヵ所があり、長城の最たりと言われる望京楼は海抜986メートル。このあたりは地勢が険しく、防御が綿密で、建築芸術が精緻で美しく、景色が雄大壮観で、古代から軍事家の争奪の目標である。長城の南側は北京市密雲県で、北側は河北省深平県である。私の家は北側である。村の年輩者の話によれば、この村の歴史がかなり古くて、ここの長城より古いそうだ。今、この村に30世

帯の人が住んで、ほとんど周という苗字で、祖先は農業で生活してきた。私は6人兄弟の二番目で、9歳の時、左足が酷く傷ついて不完全になった。1985年中学校卒業のまま家に帰る。当時は金山嶺の修復時期にあたり、私は身体障害のままほかの人と一緒に長城修復労働に参加した。修復に使うれんが、石灰、水、石……ほとんどが人力で長城に運んできた。それで、長城建築工事の規模の広大とその中にみちた苦難が分かった。長城は中華民族の血と漢の結晶だと言われているが、これはまさに真心をこめた話だと思う。

1986年の春、生活に迫られて、40元で中古品のカモメ印のカメラを買って写真をとり始めた。このカメラを持って狂うように喜んだ。村の人も特別な眼をかけてくれた。最初は彼らを写真に収めたが、長城観光業の発展に従って、観光客のために取り始めた。

1987年中国の万里の長城は世界文化遺産に選ばれた。私の故郷にある長城の知名度もますます高くなった。中国、海外の芸術家たちは創作にやってくる。私は写真界の友達が大勢できた。彼たちの啓発と助けのおかげで、私は長城風光をとり試した。やがて、《遼寧青年》雑誌の表紙に私の作品を刊行した。嬉しい気持ちで長城にまた登って、長城の後代としての責任は歴史に残ったこの貴重な遺産を写真で記録することだから、これからより多く、より良い作品を撮影しなければならないと黙想した。あれ以来、春夏秋冬を問わず、私は始終して、長城にがじりついてきた。長城を撮影することは私のこの生活の宿望である。長城は私に知恵と力を与えてくれたのだ。私は一人の農民の子供からプロの写真家に成長したのだ。私は自分の郷里を歌う為に、祖国悠々の文化を宏揚する為に、力の及ぶ限りのことをやっているだけである。五年前から写真家を出版したい考えはあるが、今はやっとこの夢がかなうようになった。長城は中国だけでなく、世界にも属すると思う。

写真集の出版において、中国写真家協会の指導者たちの関心と支持と、著名写真家の陳長芬先生の厚愛とをいただいた。編集において、陳先生は寝食を忘れて、大きな心血を注いでくださった。また、私の啓蒙先生である東風先生の長い間の御関心と御支持にも感謝の意を表したいと思う。写真同志である承徳市の衣志堅先生、李文全先生、承徳市教育書店の張国先生が多大な協力をし、長城会社の指導者が写真集の出版に関心をよせ、各界の友人が撮影の道に歩む私に絶えず営養と力を注いでくださった。ここにあわせて衷心より感謝する。

J'habite dans un village appelé Erdaoliang aux pieds de la Grande Muraille Jinshanling, Je peux voir la Muraille de la fenêtre de ma maison. Quand j'étais petit j'écoutais souvent les personnes âgées de mon village raconter des histoires de la Muraille.

Les tronçons Gubeikou, Jinshanling et Simatai de la Grande Muraille construits dans la dynastie des Ming sont reliés entre eux d'ouest en est d'une longueur de 30 kilomètres avec 12 passes importantes,5 tours de feu d'alarme, 118 tours de combat et la plus haute tour de guet de toute la Grande Muraille, la Tour Wangjinglou de 986 mètres de haut. Cette partie de la Grande Muraille fut position stratégique pour les combattants de l'époque à cause de son importance géographique, sa construction imposante et ses installations défensives rigoureuses. Au sud de la Muraille est le district Miyun relevant de la ville de Beijing, et au nord est le district Luanping de la Province du Hebei. Selon les personnes âgées locales, mon village, situant au nord extérieur de la Muraille, a une histoire qui remonte très loin, plus ancienne que la Muraille. Il y a actuellement une trentaine de familles paysannes vivant dans ce village et la plupart d'entre elles sont de même nom de famille Zhou. Je suis le deuxième enfant de ma famille avec cinq frères et soeurs. A l'âge de 9 ans je me suis blessé la jambe gauche et devenu boiteux. A la sortie de l'école secondaire en 1985, j'ai participé aux travaux de restauration de la Grande Muraille Jinshanling avec de nombreux travailleurs. C'est à ce-moment-là que j'ai commencé à comprendre l'importance et dureté des travaux de construction et restauration de la Muraille. La plupart de matériaux de construction tels que briques, chaux et l'eau sont transportés à dos par les hommes. On dit que la Grande Muraille est la cristallisation du sang et sueur de la nation chinoise. Mes expériences m'enseignent que c'est un témoignage du fond du coeur.

En été 1986 pour gagner la vie j'ai pensé à la photographie et acheté un appreil-photo de marque Haiou de seconde main pour 40 RMB. Comme j'étais extasié et aussi étaient les gens du village! Je prenais des photos pour eux et plus tard pour les touristes qui étaient de plus en plus nombreux à venir visiter ce site de la Grande Muraille.

Quand la Grande Muraille de dix milles Li a été classée parmi la liste du patrimoine culturel mondial en 1987, la Muraille de mon village connaissait plus de notoriété et attirait beaucouop d'artistes chinois et étrangers venant ici les uns après les autres pour chercher des sources de création. C'est ainsi que j'ai fait connaissance de nombreux photographes qui m'ont beaucoup inspiré et aidé. J'ai commencé à prendre des photos du paysage de la Muraille et me suis réjoui peu après de voir publiées sur la couverture de la revue Jeunesse de Liaoning quelques de mes oeuvres. Je suis remonté sur la Muraille avec plein de joie en

me disant de produire plus de belles photos, puisque je suis fils de la Grande Muraille et c'est ma responsabilité de camper sur la Muraille en toutes saisons pour l'enregistrer à travers mon appreil. C'est une volonté de vie à moi. La Muraille m'a donné la sagesse et la puissance et m'a fait devenir un photographe professionnel d'un fils de paysan. C'est ce que je peux faire en retour pour chanter mon pays natal et glorifier de longues histoires et cultures de ma patrie. J'a déjà eu l'idée de faire paraître cet album il y a 5 ans et enfin vu mon rêve réalisé aujourd'hui. La Grande Muraille appartient non seulement à la Chine mais aussi au monde entier.

L'apparition de cet album a bénéficié de soin et d'aide des dirigeants de l'Association chinoise des Photographes, surtout du soutien vigoureux du grand photographe Monsieur Chen Changfen qui a déployé toutes ses forces pour la mise en oeuvre. Mes sincères remerciements vont aussi au Groupe Jinglida de Techniques photographiques, à Monsieur Zhai Dongfeng, aux Messieurs Yi Zhijian et Li Wenquan de Chengde, à Monsieur Zhang Guo de la Librairie d'Education de Chengde pour leur plein concours, aussi aux dirigeants de la Société Grande Muraille pour leur grand souci, ainsi qu'à tous les amis qui m'ont appris et soutenu dans ma voie photographique.

2005.3